FlyHigh

Activity Book

2

Jeanne Perrett   Charlotte Covill

Contents

Lesson	Page

Alphabet

a b c d e f g h i j k l

1 **Copy.**

a _a_ ....   A _A_ ....   g ....   G ....
b ....   B ....   h ....   H ....
c ....   C ....   i ....   I ....
d ....   D ....   j ....   J ....
e ....   E ....   k ....   K ....
f ....   F ....   l ....   L ....

2 **Match.**

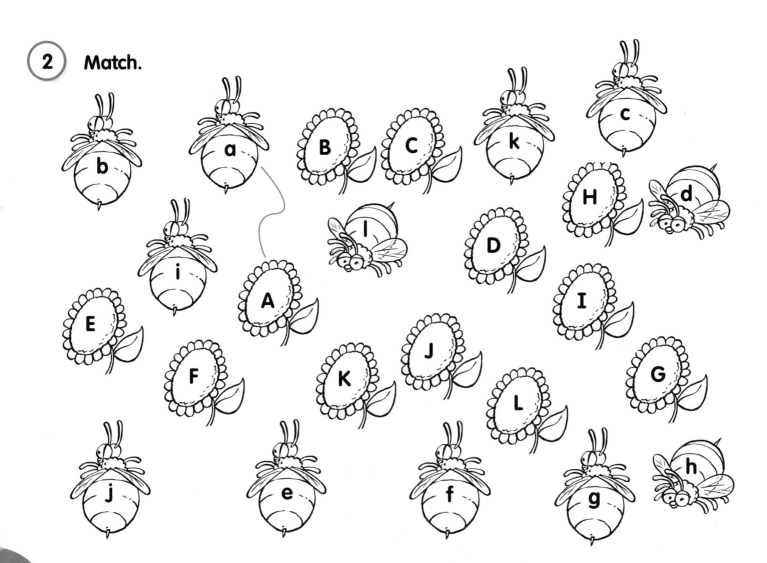

3 Complete.

a b _c_ d ..... f .... i l

.... C ..... E ..... G H ..... J K .....

4 Write and say.

1 _a_pple

2 .....ear

3 .....at

4 .....og

5 .....lephant

6 .....lower

7 .....oat

8 .....ippo

9 .....nsect

10 .....elly

11 .....angaroo

12 .....ion

1 Copy.

m _m_	M _M_	s	S ....
n	N	t	T ....
o	O	u	U ....
p	P	v	V ....
q	Q	w	W ....
r	R		

2 Match.

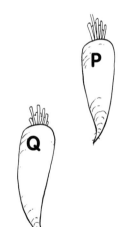
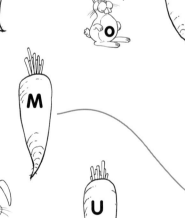
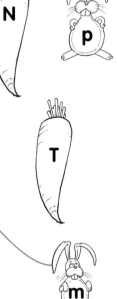

3 **Complete.**

m n ..... p ..... r ..... u v .....

M N O ..... Q ..... S T .... W

4 **Write and say.**

1 _m_ onkey

2 ....est

3 ....ctopus

4 ....enguin

5 ....ueen

6 ....abbit

7 ....nake

8 ....iger

9 ....mbrella

10 ....ulture

11 ....hale

Alphabet

x y z

(1) Copy.

x _x_   X _X_

y ....   Y ....

z ....   Z ....

(2) Write and say.

1 fo _x_   **2** ....o-.....o   **3** ....ebra

(3) Complete.

a b .... f .... i .... n

.... q .... v ....

A .... D .... H .... K ....

O .... S .... W .... Z

4 Find and circle. Then say.

1

```
k a n g a r o o
q d v y a c p j
y x u e p a e r
o l l p p r n a
y i t a l b g b
o q u e e n u b
u m r s b p i i
e l e p h a n t
```

8

2

7

3

4

5

6

5 Match and complete. Then say.

1 _b_ ear

2 ....oat

3 ....nsect

4 ....onkey

5 ....nake

6 ....mbrella

7 ....ippo

8 ....ebra

Colours

1   **Read and colour.**

red
black
green
orange
purple
yellow

blue
brown
pink
grey
white

2   **Find and circle. Then colour.**

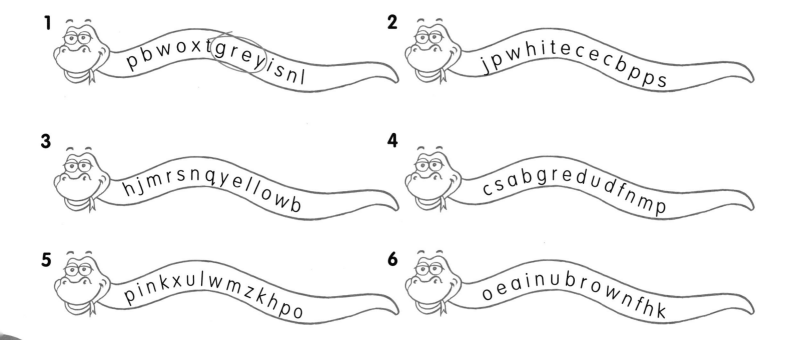

1   p b w o x t g r e y i s n l

2   j p w h i t e c e c b p p s

3   h j m r s n q y e l l o w b

4   c s a b g r e d u d f n m p

5   p i n k x u l w m z k h p o

6   o e a i n u b r o w n f h k

Numbers

1 Circle.

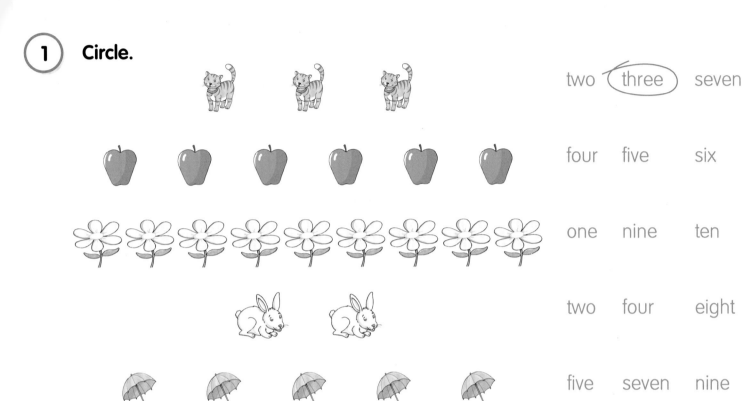

two	(three)	seven
four	five	six
one	nine	ten
two	four	eight
five	seven	nine

2 Count and write.

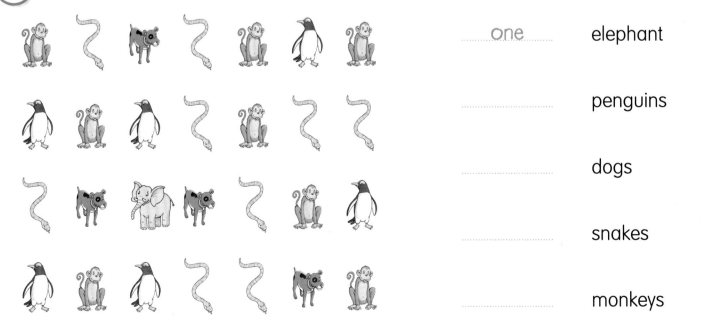

one	elephant
	penguins
	dogs
	snakes
	monkeys

1 It's a school!

1 Look and circle.

What's this?

1 It's a (bag) / book.
2 It's a pencil / pen.
3 It's a book / pen.

4 It's a pen / rubber.
5 It's a book / pencil.

2 Find and circle.

bagpencilbookpenrubber

3 **Match.**

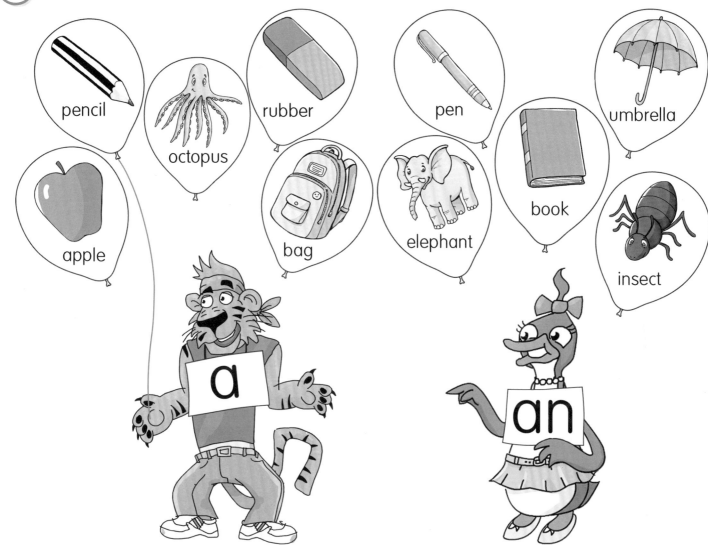

pencil

octopus

apple

rubber

bag

pen

elephant

book

umbrella

insect

a

an

4 **Look and write.**

1 What's this?
It's ..... a pencil ..... .

2 What's this?
It's ....

3 What's this?
It's ....

4 What's this?
It's ....

5 What's this?
It's ....

6 What's this?
It's ....

2 Spell octopus.

1 Match.

1 Be quiet, please.   **2** Spell 'dog', please.   **3** Write 'cat', please.

a    **b**   **c**

2 Read and colour.

bag = blue   book = red   pen = pink
rubber = white   board = green   chair = brown

3 **Look at Exercise 2 and write.**

What colour is it?

1 The *board* is green.
2 The .... is red.
3 The .... is white.

4 The .... is pink.
5 The .... is brown.
6 The .... is blue.

4 **Read and draw. Then colour.**

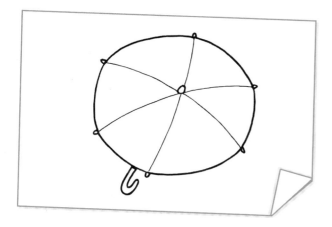

1 What's this? It's an umbrella.
The umbrella is red and blue.

2 What's this? It's a flower.
The flower is orange and yellow.

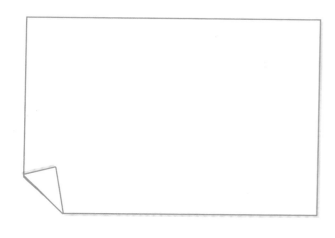

3 What's this? It's a pencil.
The pencil is pink and grey.

4 What's this? It's a snake.
The snake is green and black.

(3) Cars and balls!

(1) Match and colour.

1

black cars

blue dolls

red balls

yellow stickers

purple crayons

pink bags

2

3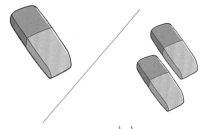

4

5

6

(2) Count and write.

1   a rubber
two rubbers

2 ....

3 ....

4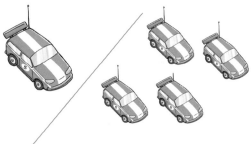
....

5
....

6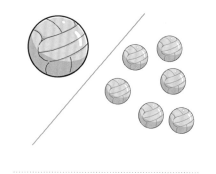
....

3 **Read and match.**

1 What are they?
   They're bears.
2 What are they?
   They're lions.
3 What are they?
   They're hippos.

4 **Write** What's this **or** What are they.

1 <u>What are they</u> ?
   They're balls.

2 _____ ?
   It's a doll.

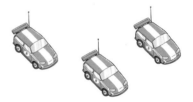

3 _____ ?
   They're cars.

4 _____ ?
   They're stickers.

5 _____ ?
   It's an elephant.

6 _____ ?
   It's a card.

5 **Write** It's a, It's an **or** They're.

1 <u>It's a</u> chair.   **2** _____ octopus.   **3** _____ crayons.

4 That's a robot!

1 **Find the presents and write.**

~~robot~~   doll   cake   watch

1 It's a robot!
Thank you!

2 ....
Thank you!

3 ....
Thank you!

4 ....
Thank you!

2 **Read and colour.**

1 This is a blue pencil.
That is a yellow pencil.

2 That is a black cat.
This is an orange cat.

3 This is a green car.
That is a red car.

3 **Write** This is **or** That is.

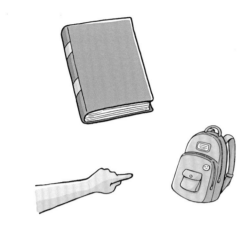

1 .....This is..... a book.
.....That is..... a bag.

2 .... a cake.
.... a robot.

3 .... a whale.
.... a penguin.

4 .... a car.
.... a doll.

4 **Match.**

1 What's this?

2 What are they?

3 What are they?

4 What's that?

a They're my presents.

b It's my birthday cake.

c That's a robot.

d They're my cards.

Happy Birthday!

Sally's Story

The frogs!

1 Choose and write.

Open the window!   Sit down, please.   ~~Close the door!~~   Stand up!

1

Close the door!

2

3

4

2 Count and write.

1 ....five........ dolls

2 .... robots

3 .... balls

4 .... crayons

3 Do the crossword.

teacher ~~book~~ window rubber door board

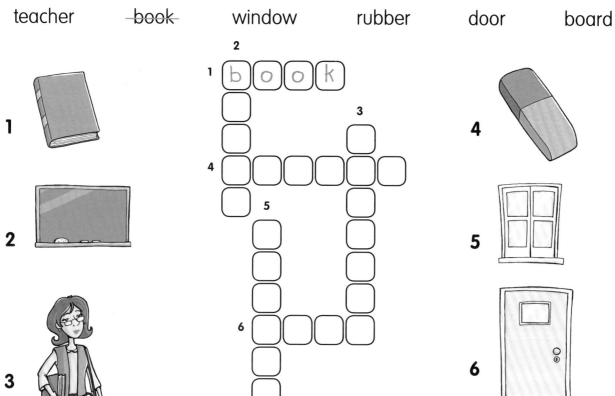

1 **b o o k**

What about you?

4 Read and colour. Then draw and write about your bag.

My name is Tag.
This is my bag.
It's blue and yellow.

My name is ....
This is *my* ....
It's ....

The FlyHigh Review ①

1 Choose and write.

Birthday   It's   is   you   ~~this~~   Spell   an

1 What's _____this_____ ?
It's _____ octopus.
_____ 'octopus', please.
o...c...t...o...p...u...s

2 Happy _____ !
This _____ your present.
_____ a pen.
Thank _____ !

2 Write.

1 _____It's a board._____
2 _____They're crayons._____
3 _____
4 _____
5 _____

3 Find, circle and match.

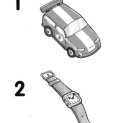

1

2

3

4

b	j	w	j	e	s	p	j	d	j
a	g	c	i	l	z	w	u	o	o
l	p	r	e	s	e	n	t	l	x
l	x	o	q	s	a	o	a	l	u
d	z	e	y	j	r	j	c	m	c
h	n	r	o	b	o	t	t	w	a
t	c	h	b	k	s	d	o	f	k
w	a	t	c	h	u	d	n	g	e
f	i	o	a	d	u	b	i	g	n
d	s	o	c	a	r	v	c	l	i

5

6

7

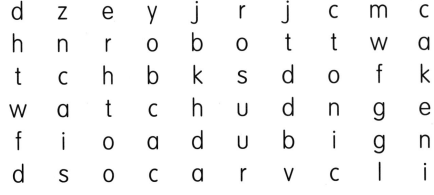

4 **Match.**

a 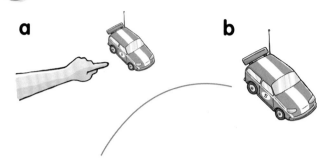 b

c d

1 This is a car. **2** That is a car. **3** This is a cat. **4** That is a cat.

5 **Circle.**

1  (Stand up, please.) /
Close the window,
please.

2 Sit down, please. /
Open the door,
please.

3 Stand up, please. /
Sit down, please.

4  Close the window,
please. /
Open the door,
please.

My English

Read and colour.

1 What's this? It's a pen. ☺ ☺ ☺
2 What are they? They're balls. ☺ ☺ ☺
3 This is a car. That is a ball. ☺ ☺ ☺
4 Stand up! Sit down! ☺ ☺ ☺

5 She's pretty.

1 Find and circle. Then match and write.

wvbrothermtdadixsisterbafamilyglmum

1 .... family ....

2 ....

3 ....

4 ....

5 ....

2 Colour the 👤 words blue and the 👤 words red.

mum   brother
sister   dad

3 Circle.

1 <u>I'm</u> / She's Patty.

2 He's / She's Chatter.

3 I'm / You're a tiger.

4 I'm / He's Tag.

5 I'm / It's an insect.

6 I'm / She's Karla.

4 Write He's or She's.

1 .....She's..... my sister.

2 .... my mum.

3 .... my dad.

4 .... my brother.

6 Is he your grandpa?

1 Find, circle and match.

1

b	r	p	v	w	s	q	g
r	o	s	i	s	t	e	r
o	y	c	a	d	h	k	a
t	i	m	u	m	g	z	n
h	m	n	b	v	d	a	d
e	s	w	i	d	f	r	p
r	g	r	a	n	d	m	a

2

3

4

5

6

2 Circle the family words.

ball pencil mum family brother

sister car

dad chair cake apple crayon

3 Write ? or .

1 Are you my friend ?

2 You are my friend

3 He's my grandpa

4 Is she your grandma

5 Am I your friend

6 It's a snake

4 **Look and circle.**

1 Is he a boy?
~~Yes, he is.~~ /
No, he isn't.

2 Is she a girl?
Yes, she is. /
No, she isn't.

3 Is she a teacher?
Yes, she is. /
No, she isn't.

4 Is he a baby?
Yes, he is. /
No, he isn't.

5 **Match.**

1 Is your name Patty?
2 Are you a girl?
3 Is Sally your friend?
4 Is Trumpet your brother?
5 Are you a teacher?
6 Is your grandma a teacher?

a Yes, I am.
b No, I'm not.
c No, he isn't.
d No, she isn't.
e Yes, it is.
f Yes, she is.

6 **Write the questions in the correct order. Then answer about you.**

1 your name / Is / Tag?   Is your name Tag?   No, it isn't.
2 Are / a boy? / you
3 you / Are / a girl?
4 a teacher? / your grandpa / Is
5 Is / pretty? / your mum

7 We're cowboys.

1 Match.

1

2

3

She's a dancer.

He's a spy.

They're clothes.

They're cowboys.

It's a box.

They're friends.

4

5

6

2 Circle.

1 (They're) / We're **boys.**

2 We're / You're **girls.**

3 We're / They're **friends.**

4 They're / You're **presents.**

3 **Choose and write.**

We're teachers.   ~~We're penguins.~~   You're grandpas.   You're cowboys.

1 We're penguins.

2 ....

3 ....

4 ....

4 **Write** We're, You're **or** They're.

1 Chatter and Tag are friends.   They're   friends.
2 My friend and I are girls.   .... girls.
3 My mum and dad are teachers.   .... teachers.
4 You and your sister are pretty.   .... pretty.
5 Patty and her sister are penguins.   .... penguins.
6 Tag and I are cowboys.   .... cowboys.

5 **Match the short forms and the long forms.**

1 I'm a boy.   **a** We are friends.
2 She's my sister.   **b** He is my dad.
3 He's my dad.   **c** You are dancers.
4 We're friends.   **d** They are teachers.
5 You're dancers.   **e** I am a boy.
6 They're teachers.   **f** She is my sister.

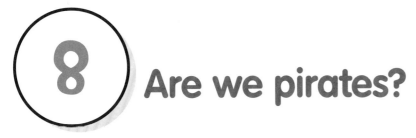

8 Are we pirates?

1 **Complete and draw.**

crown   dancer   teacher   ~~spy~~   king   queen

1

2

3

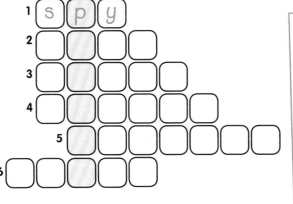

1 | s | p | y |

4    **5**   **6**

2 **Write.**

1 They're _dancers_ .   **2** We're _____ .   **3** They're _____ .

3 **Write ? or .**

1 They are dancers ____
2 Are we cowboys ____
3 Are you queens ____

4 You are clowns ____
5 Are they pirates ____
6 We are kings ____

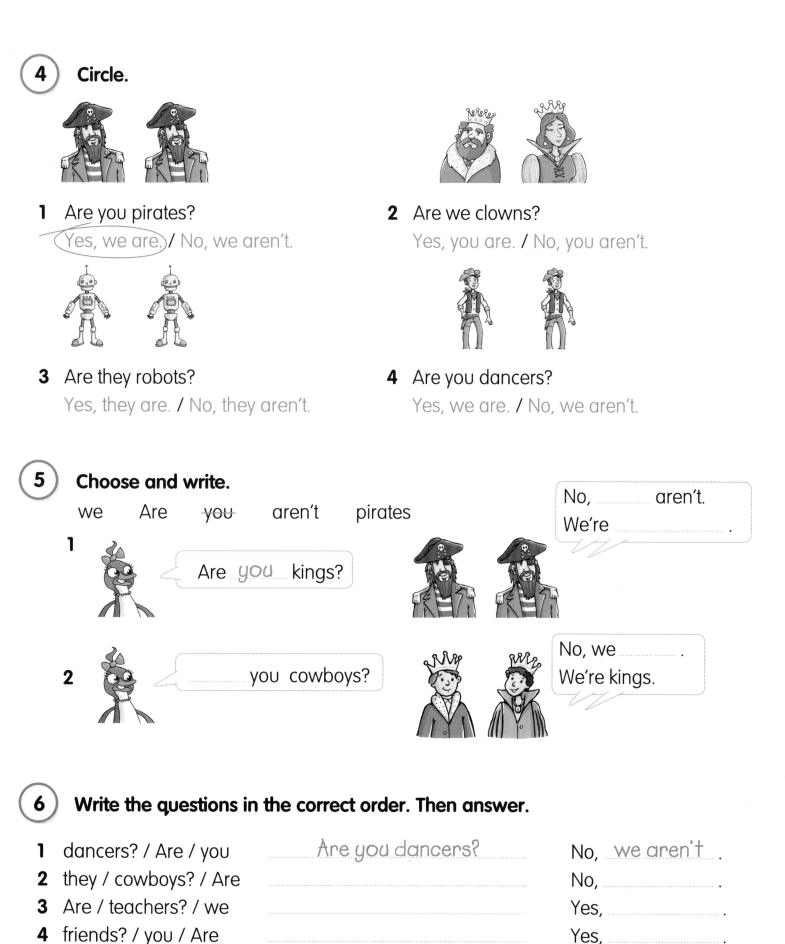

4 Circle.

1 Are you pirates?
Yes, we are. / No, we aren't.

2 Are we clowns?
Yes, you are. / No, you aren't.

3 Are they robots?
Yes, they are. / No, they aren't.

4 Are you dancers?
Yes, we are. / No, we aren't.

5 Choose and write.

we   Are   ~~you~~   aren't   pirates

1

Are you kings?

No, ... aren't.
We're ....

2

.... you cowboys?

No, we ....
We're kings.

6 Write the questions in the correct order. Then answer.

1 dancers? / Are / you   Are you dancers?   No, we aren't .

2 they / cowboys? / Are   ....   No, ...

3 Are / teachers? / we   ....   Yes, ...

4 friends? / you / Are   ....   Yes, ...

Sally's Story
The grey duck

1 Choose and write.

No, I'm not.   Yes, you are!   We're swans.   ~~Hello, Mum.~~   No, she isn't.

1

Hello. I'm your mum.

Hello, Mum.

2

Hello, are you my mum?

....

3

Is she my sister?

....

4

Am I a swan?

....
....

2 Match.

1    It's a duck.   **2**
It's a swan.

3   He's happy.   **4**
He's sad.

5   It's big.   **6**
It's small.

3 Find the odd one out. Write.

1 brother	father	(small)	mum	*small*
2 mother	sad	dad	sister	
3 happy	swan	duck	vulture	
4 grandma	grandpa	brother	big	

What about you?

4 Read and write is, are, He's or She's. Then draw and write about your family.

I'm Mary.
This ___is___ a picture of my family.
My family _____ small.
This _____ my brother, Tom.
_____ eleven.
This _____ my mum. _____ pretty.
This _____ my dad. _____ nice.
My grandma and grandpa _____
in the picture too.

I'm _____ .
This is a picture of *my family*.
This _____ .
This _____ .
This _____ .

① Write.

	Short form	Long form
1	I'm	I am
2		you are
3		he is
4	she's	

	Short form	Long form
5	it's	
6		we are
7	they're	

② Match.

1 I'm a   **a** dancer?
2 He's an   **b** pirates.
3 Is she a   **c** cowboy.
4 Are they   **d** octopus?
5 We're   **e** elephant.
6 Are you an   **f** swans?

③ Choose and write.

She isn't   I'm   It isn't   You're   They aren't   ~~We're~~

1 _We're_ brothers.

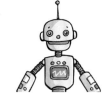

2 .... a doll.

3 .... a king.

4 .... ducks.

5 .... my grandpa.

6 .... a spy.

4 Choose and write.

No, they aren't.   No, he isn't.   ~~Yes, she is.~~   Yes, they are.   No, I'm not.

1 Is Sally a girl?   Yes, she is.
2 Are Karla and Patty friends?
3 Is Chatter a baby?
4 Are Trumpet and Tag small?
5 Are you a teacher?

5 Choose and write.

~~mum~~   ~~clown~~   king   grandma   dancer   grandpa
dad   ~~pirate~~   cowboy   spy   sister

1 Me   **2**   **3**   **4**   **5**   **6**

1 I'm a pirate.   **4**
2 My mum is a clown.   **5**
3   **6**

My English

Read and colour.

1 Is she your sister? Yes, she is. / No, she isn't.
2 Are they pirates? Yes, they are. / No, they aren't.

9 It's his kite.

1 **Find and circle. Then match and write.**

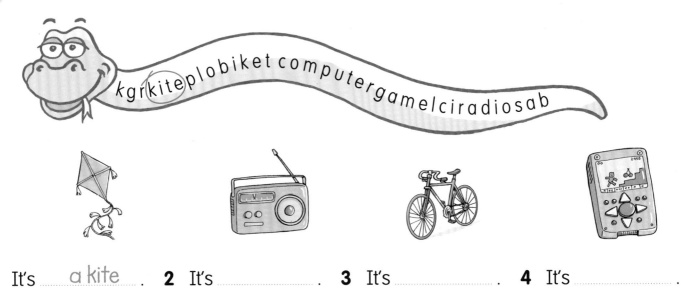

kgr(kite)plobiket computergamelciradiosab

1 It's ..... a kite ..... . **2** It's .... **3** It's .... **4** It's ....

2 **Find and complete.**

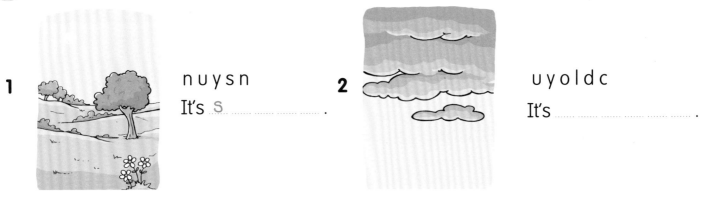

1 n u y s n
It's s ....

2 u y o l d c
It's ....

3 **Circle.**

1 He's a boy. Her / (His) kite is yellow.

2 She's a girl. My / Her doll is old.

3 I'm a tiger. My / Its bike is new.

4 It's a computer game. Its / Your name is Flying Robots.

5 You're my friend. This is your / his book.

4   **Match and write.**

1   I'm Patty.
2   You're Karla.
3   He's Chatter.
4   She's Sally.
5   It's Max.

a   Its name is ....
b   His name is ....
c   Her name is ....
d   My name is .... Patty ....
e   Your name is ....

5   **Write His or Her and colour.**

1   ....His.... kite is red.
2   .... radio is black.
3   .... computer game is green.
4   .... bike is blue.

5   .... robot is grey.
6   .... ball is orange.
7   .... books are pink.

10 They're our toys.

1 Choose and write.

clothes / (toys)   bikes / rollerblades   train / car

1 They're _toys_ .   **2** They're _____ .   **3** It's a _____ .

2 Write. Use slow or fast.

1 Penguins _are slow_ .   **2** Tigers _____ .

3 Hippos _____ .   **4** Dogs _____ .

3 Find the odd one out. Write.

1	rollerblades	computer game	kite	(grandma)	_grandma_
2	swan	radio	kite	doll	
3	slow	prize	fast	old	
4	bike	train	winner	car	

4 Read and match.

It's our cat. It's their rabbit.

It's our umbrella. It's their yo-yo.

They're our rollerblades. It's their car.

1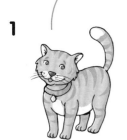
2
3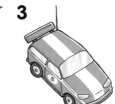
4
5
6

5 Write our, your or their.

1 This is my brother and this is ....our.... mum.
2 Are you kings? Here are .... crowns.
3 Sam and Ella are happy. It's .... birthday.
4 We're friends and .... names are Joe and Laura.
5 They're sisters. These are .... clothes.
6 Are you the winners? Here are .... prizes.

6 Circle.

1 We / (Our) names are Maria and Anna.
2 We / Our are sisters.
3 They / Their are our brothers.
4 They / Their bikes are fast.
5 You / Your are our friends.
6 You / Your kite is blue and white.

11 I've got a pet.

1 Choose and write.

arm   body   feet   wing   hand   ~~head~~   leg

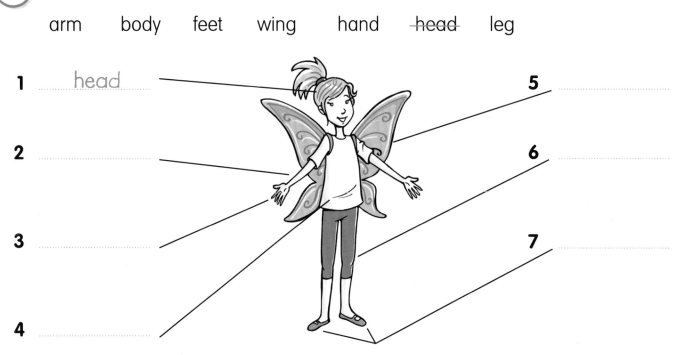

1 head
2
3
4

5
6
7

2 Match and colour.

a

b

c

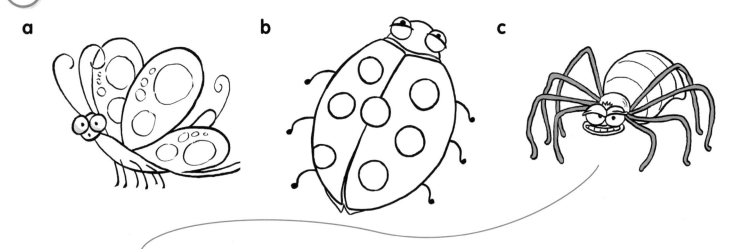

1 It's got a blue body. It's got eight legs and feet.

2 It's got six legs. It's got a long brown body. It's got a small head. It's got two beautiful green wings.

3 It's got a black head. It's got a red body with seven black spots. It's got six legs and feet.

3 **Match the short forms and the long forms.**

1 I've got a pet.
2 You've got two legs.
3 She's got an insect.
4 It's got six legs.
5 We've got hands and feet.
6 They've got wings.

a They have got wings.
b It has got six legs.
c We have got hands and feet.
d I have got a pet.
e You have got two legs.
f She has got an insect.

4 **Write 've got or 's got and match.**

1
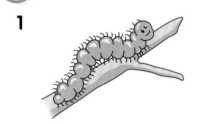

2

3

She 's got a cat.

They _____ a dog.

He _____ a rabbit.

We _____ a goat.

I _____ an insect.

It _____ lots of legs.

4

5

6

5 **Write He's / She's / It's got or We've / You've / They've got.**

1 Patty has got a pet.   She's got a pet.
2 The insect has got wings.   _____ wings.
3 Tag and Trumpet have got four legs.   _____ four legs.
4 My brother and I have got a cat.   _____ a cat.
5 You and your sister have got a dog.   _____ a dog.
6 Tag has got an orange and black body. _____ an orange and black body.

Have we got all the insects?

1 **Do the crossword.**

eyes   mouth   ears   ~~nose~~   head   hair

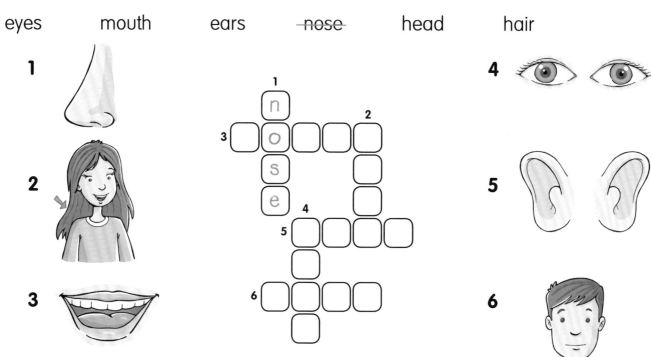

2 **Read and match.**

a   b   c   d

1 He's got big feet. He hasn't got big hands.   _d_

2 She's got big eyes. She hasn't got a big nose.   _____

3 She's got a big mouth. She hasn't got big ears.   _____

4 He's got big ears. He hasn't got big eyes.   _____

3 Write has got or hasn't got.

1 A butterfly ....has got........ wings.
2 A snake .... legs.
3 An octopus .... eight legs.
4 A monkey .... hands and arms.
5 A penguin .... hands.

4 Write ? or .

1 He's got brown eyes .....
2 Have you got black hair ......
3 Has she got a pink mouth ......
4 They've got big ears ......

5 It's got beautiful wings ......
6 Have they got lots of legs ......
7 Has it got arms ......
8 I've got blue eyes ......

5 Match.

1 Has Tag got lots of friends?
2 Has Sally got a hair slide?
3 Have you got a big family?
4 Has Trumpet got a computer game?
5 Have they got two sisters?
6 Have we got a prize?

a Yes, you have.
b Yes, he has.
c No, he hasn't.
d No, they haven't.
e Yes, she has.
f No, I haven't.

6 Write the questions in the correct order. Then answer about you.

1 you / Have / got / a / computer game?
   Have you got a computer game?
   ....

2 rollerblades? / got / Have / you
   ....
   ....

3 your / got / mum / radio? / a / Has
   ....
   ....

4 dad / car? / got / Has / your / a
   ....
   ....

Circus boy!

1 Read, choose and write.

's got   've got   ~~have got~~   isn't   fast   strong   hands

1 The clowns *have got* long arms and legs.

2 Sam _____ short arms and legs.

3 The dancers have got beautiful feet and _____ .

4 The monkeys are very _____ .

5 The elephants are _____ .

6 They _____ big trunks.

7 Sam _____ fast or strong. But look! He's a star!

2 Find the odd one out. Write.

1	long	arms	hair	legs	*long*
2	feet	ears	big	trunk	
3	clown	funny	boy	dancer	
4	hands	eyes	beautiful	hair	

3 Choose and write.

old   ~~short~~   long   strong

 **1**  **2**  **3**  **4**

It's _____short_____ . It's _____ . It's _____ . It's _____ .

What about you?

4 Read and circle. Then draw and write about you.

My name's Vicky.
I've got (brown) / green eyes.
I've got long / short brown hair.
I've got a big / small nose and a big /
small mouth.
I'm happy / sad.

My name's _____ .
I've got _____ eyes.
I've got _____ hair.
I've got _____
and _____ .
I'm _____ .

The FlyHigh Review ③

1 **Choose and write.**

eyes   ~~legs~~   ears   hands   arms   nose   feet   ~~hair~~

My head

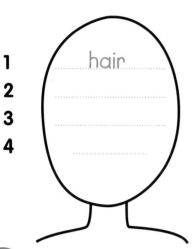

1 hair
2 ....
3 ....
4 ....

My body

1 legs
2 ....
3 ....
4 ....

2 **Match.**

1 old   **a** short
2 long   **b** new

3 happy   **c** sunny
4 cloudy   **d** sad

3 **Match. Then choose and write.**

his   ~~my~~   her   our   their

1 I've got a

2 We've got a

3 She's got

4 They've got a

5 He's got a

a It's .... kite.

b It's .... train.

c It's ....my.... radio.

d It's .... computer game.

e They're .... rollerblades.

4 Choose and write.

~~'ve got~~   haven't got   have got   's got   hasn't got   haven't got

1 I ....'ve got.... a bike.
2 Helen and Chris .... a kite.
3 They .... a train.

4 Helen .... a hair slide.
5 Chris .... computer game.
6 I .... a kite.

5 Answer about you. Tick (✓) or cross (✗) and write. Use I've got or I haven't got.

1 a bag ....
2 a ball ....
3 a computer game ....
4 a watch ....
5 a bike ....
6 a robot ....

My English

Read and colour.

1 I've got a radio. My radio is new.
2 Have you got blue eyes? Yes, I have. / No, I haven't.

13 There's a town.

1 Complete.

1 It's a sw i mm i ng p oo l.

2 It's a h___s___.

3 They're ch__ld_____.

4 It's a pl_____gr_____nd.

5 It's a tr_____.

6 It's a r__v_____.

2 Write and colour.

1 There are two pink ____houses____.   **4** There's a blue _____.
2 There are four green _____.   **5** There are eight red _____.
3 There are three _____.

3 Circle.

1 There's a river.   yes / (no)
2 There's a pool.   yes / no
3 There's a swan.   yes / no
4 There are lots of trees.   yes / no
5 There are three children.   yes / no

4 Look at Exercise 3. Circle.

1 There's / There are **a park.**   **4** There's / There are **lots of flowers.**
2 There's / There are **a nest.**   **5** There's / There are **five trees.**
3 There's / There are **two children.**

5 Look at Exercise 3 and write.

	a big	dogs.	**1**	There's a big boy.
There's	two	girl.	**2**	
There are	a small	ducks.	**3**	
	a pretty	rabbit.	**4**	
	three	boy.	**5**	

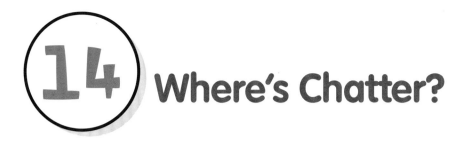

14 Where's Chatter?

1 **Choose and write.**

slide   ~~swing~~   treehouse   climbing frame

1 ....swing.......

2 ....

3 ....

4 ....
  ....

2 **Read and draw.**

1   The ball is under the swing.

2   The doll is on the slide.

3   The cat is under the climbing frame.

4   The kite is in the tree.

5   The butterfly is on the climbing frame.

3 **Choose and write.**

in   on   under   ~~next to~~

1 The rabbits are _____next to_____ the flower.
2 The cat is _____ the chair.
3 The apples are _____ the bag.
4 The dog is _____ the umbrella.

4 **Look at Exercise 3. Then choose and write. Use** Where's? **or** Where are?.

the book   the frogs   ~~the butterfly~~   the radio   the insects

1 _____Where's the butterfly?_____ It's on the flower.
2 _____ It's next to the dog.
3 _____ They're in the pool.
4 _____ It's under the chair.
5 _____ They're on the umbrella.

15 I can sing.

1 Find, circle and write.

1

2

3

w	s	r	g	t	y	s
c	l	i	m	b	t	w
o	y	d	a	d	h	i
j	i	e	k	l	z	m
u	p	l	a	y	d	a
m	s	w	s	i	n	g
p	g	q	a	x	c	g

4

5

6

1 climb   3 ....   5 ....

2 ....   4 ....   6 ....

2 Match.

1 We can sing   a in the pool.
2 We can climb   b a song.
3 We can swim   c the guitar.
4 We can ride   d the tree.
5 We can play   e a bike.

3 Look and write He can, She can or They can.

1 He can .... climb.
2 .... sing.
3 .... play the guitar.
4 .... swim.
5 .... ride a bike.

4 **Choose and write.**

ride a bike   ~~sing~~   play the guitar   ride a bike   swim

My name's Paula. I can (**1**) ....sing........, (**2**) ....

and (**3**) ....

My friend, Alice, can also (**4**) .... and she

can (**5**) ....

5 **Write and match.**

1 They/swim   ....They can swim.........

2 He/jump   ....

3 It/climb   ....

4 You/sing   ....

6 **Write about you.**

1 I can ....write............ .   **3** ....

2 I can ....   **4** ....

16 Can you skip?

1 **Do the crossword.**

~~swim~~   fly   run   skip   walk   carry   climb

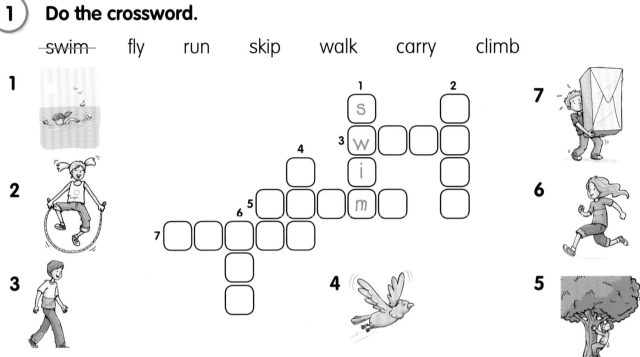

1

2

3

4

5

6

7

2 **Look and write** Yes, he/she can **or** No, he/she can't.

1 Can she dance?

Yes, she can.

2 Can he sing?

3 Can she ride a bike?

4 Can he rollerblade?

5 Can he swim?

6 Can she do a handstand?

3 **Choose, write and answer.**

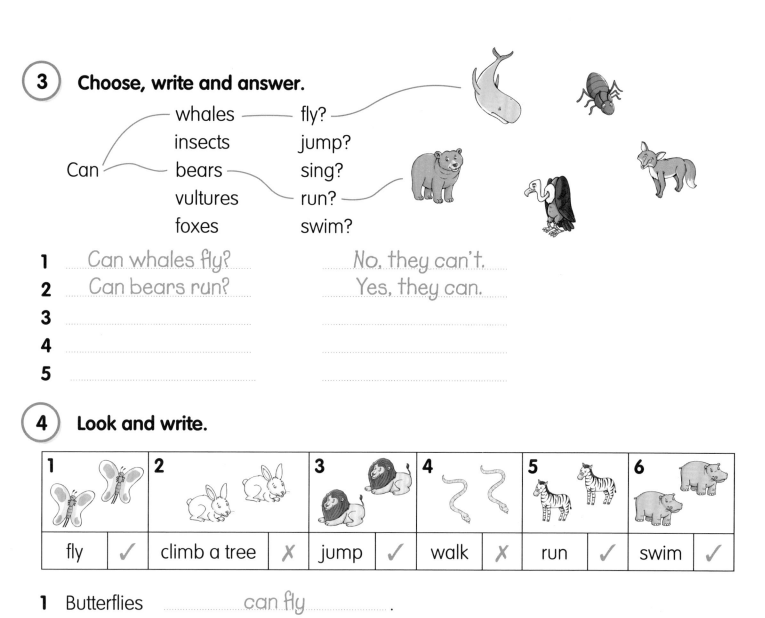

Can — whales — fly?
insects — jump?
bears — sing?
vultures — run?
foxes — swim?

1 Can whales fly?   No, they can't.
2 Can bears run?   Yes, they can.
3 ....
4 ....
5 ....

4 **Look and write.**

1		2		3		4		5		6	
fly	✓	climb a tree	✗	jump	✓	walk	✗	run	✓	swim	✓

1 Butterflies ....can fly.........
2 Rabbits ....
3 Lions ....
4 Snakes ....
5 Zebras ....
6 Hippos ....

5 **Write about you. Use can or can't.**

1 I/do a handstand ....
2 I/swim ....
3 I/rollerblade ....
4 My mum/ride a bike ....
5 My dad/play the guitar ....

Where's my mobile phone?

1 **Choose and write.**

It isn't under the computer.   ~~I can't find my mobile phone.~~
It's in his bed!   It isn't on the table.

1

> I can't find my mobile phone.

2

> ....

3

> ....

4

> ....

2 **Choose and write.**

bag   haven't   isn't   in   ~~got~~   can't

Mum: James, have you (**1**) .... got .... my mobile phone?
James: No, I (**2**) ....
Mum: I (**3**) .... find my phone.
James: Is it in the cupboard?
Mum: No, it (**4**) ....
James: Is it (**5**) .... the bookcase?
Mum: No, it isn't. Here it is. It's in my (**6**) .... !

3 Match.

1	There's a computer	next to	the cupboard.
2	There's a guitar	in	the desk.
3	There are rollerblades	under	the bookcase.
4	There are clothes	on	the bed.

What about you?

4 Read and write. Then draw and write about you.

In my bedroom, there's a .... bed .... , a cupboard, a bookcase, a .... and a chair. There's a .... on the desk.
There are lots of books in the ....

In my bedroom, there's ....
....
There's ....
There are ....

(1) Find the odd one out. Write.

1 town	shop	house	(rollerblades)	*rollerblades*
2 climbing frame	cupboard	slide	swing	....
3 mobile phone	school	playground	swimming pool	....
4 bookcase	bus	table	bed	....

(2) Look, choose and write.

~~in~~   on   under   next to   in

1 There are clothes ......in...... the cupboard.

2 There's a computer .... the desk.

3 There's a bookcase .... the desk.

4 There are books .... the bookcase.

5 There's a bus .... the bed.

(3) Look at Exercise 2. Circle.

1 Is there a table next to the bed? (Yes, there is.)/ No, there isn't.

2 Is there a book under the bed? Yes, there is. / No, there isn't.

3 Is there a doll on the bed? Yes, there is. / No, there isn't.

4 Are there clothes on the desk? Yes, there are. / No, there aren't.

5 Are there books in the bookcase? Yes, there are. / No, there aren't.

4 Write.

1	He can't ride a bike.	6	
2	She can run.	7	
3		8	
4		9	
5		10	

5 Write about you.

1 I can ....

2 I can't ....

My English

Read and colour.

1 In my bedroom, there's a cupboard. There are two beds.

2 Where's the book? It's on the table.

3 Can you swim? Yes, I can. / No, I can't.

17 I like breakfast.

1 **Complete and draw.**

milk   orange   honey   octopus   ~~egg~~   bread   hungry   apple

1    **2**   **3**   **4**

1   e g g
2
3
4
5
6
7
8

5    **6**   **7**   **8**

2 **Circle and write.**

1 My friend and I like   .   (We) / They .... like apples ....

2 My friend and I like   .   We / They ....

3 Chatter and Tag like .   We / They ....

4 My mum and dad like .   We / They ....

3 **Circle.**

1 I like / don't like burgers.

2 I like / don't like milk.

3 We like / don't like honey.

4 They like / don't like eggs.

4 **Look and write. Use like or don't like.**

1		2		3		4		5		6	
milk	✓	honey	✗	bread	✓	apples	✓	jelly	✗	burgers	✓

1 Cats .... like milk ....   **4** Rabbits ....
2 Frogs ....   **5** Lions ....
3 Ducks ....   **6** Children ....

5 **Write about you. Use like or don't like.**

1 I .... milk.   **3** I .... jelly.
2 I .... apples.   **4** I .... burgers.

18 Do you like fish, Patty?

1 Choose and write.

fish honey pizza ~~soup~~ chicken egg salad orange

1 .... soup ....

2 ....

3 ....

4 ....

5 ....

2 What's missing in Exercise 1? Draw and write.

1 ....   **2** ....   **3** ....

3 Write about you. Answer *Yes, I do* or *No, I don't.*

1 Do you like chicken? ....   **4** Do you like pizza? ....

2 Do you like salad? ....   **5** Do you like fish? ....

3 Do you like soup? ....

4 Write **?** or **.**

1 I like fish ......**.**......

2 Do you like apples ....

3 They don't like honey ....

4 Do they like pizza ....

5 Write *Yes, they do* **or** *No, they don't.*

1 Do they like eggs? .... *Yes, they do.* ....

2 Do they like oranges? ....

3 Do they like pizza? ....

4 Do they like honey? ....

5 Do they like fish? ....

6 Do they like cake? ....

6 Write the questions in the correct order. Then answer about you.

1 honey? / you / Do / like

.... *Do you like honey?* ....

2 Do / pizza? / your friends / like

....

3 like / Do / fish? / you

....

4 like / your friends / Do / computer games?

....

5 your dad and mum / like / Do / chicken?

....

19 He gets up at seven o'clock.

1 **Choose and write.**

She has breakfast.   She goes to school.   She cleans her teeth.   ~~She gets up.~~

1  .... She gets up. ....

2  ....

3  ....

4  ....

2 **Choose and write the correct form.**

have   go   ~~get up~~   clean   play   like

1 My name's Maria. I .... get up .... at seven o'clock.

My friend, Sue, ... gets up .... at eight o'clock.

2 I .... to school at eight o'clock.

Sue .... to school at nine o'clock.

3 I .... lunch at one o'clock.

Sue .... lunch at two o'clock.

4 I .... fish and salad.

Sue .... burgers.

5 I .... the guitar every day.

Sue .... computer games every day.

6 I .... my teeth at eight o'clock.

Sue .... her teeth at nine o'clock.

(3) **Write about you. Answer** Yes, I do **or** No, I don't.

1 Do you get up at seven o'clock? ....

2 Do you go to school at nine o'clock? ....

3 Do you have lunch at one o'clock? ....

4 Do you go to the park every day? ....

5 Do you swim every day? ....

6 Do you play computer games every day? ....

(4) **Read and draw.**

1 It's one o'clock.   **2** It's three o'clock.   **3** It's five o'clock.   **4** It's nine o'clock.

(5) **Write.**

1 It's two o'clock.   **2** ....   **3** ....

4 ....   **5** ....   **6** ....

20 Does Rob go to the zoo every day?

1 **Circle. Then complete.**

1 It's M o nday.
2 It's T .... sday.
3 It's W .... dn .... day.

4 It's Th .... day.
5 It's F .... day.
6 It's S ...... t .... day.

2 **Look and tick (✓) or cross (✗).**

1 Does Anna clean her teeth at seven o'clock every day? ✓
2 Does Anna have breakfast at seven o'clock every day?
3 Does Anna play the guitar at five o'clock every day?
4 Does Anna go to bed at nine o'clock every day?

3 **Write** Yes, he does **or** No, he doesn't.

	Monday	Tuesday	Wednesday	Thursday	Friday	Saturday

1 Does Sam play basketball on Monday?   Yes, he does.
2 Does he go the park on Tuesday?
3 Does he swim on Wednesday?
4 Does he play his guitar on Thursday?
5 Does he ride his bike on Friday?
6 Does he go to school on Saturday?

4 **Write** likes **or** doesn't like.

1   ☺   Sam   likes burgers .

2   ☹   Sam .

3   ☺   Sam .

4   ☹   Sam .

Sally's Story
Superboy

1 **Read and answer.**

1 Does Superboy help old people on Monday?

Yes, he does.

2 Does he visit his grandma and grandpa on Tuesday?

3 Does he do his homework on Wednesday?

4 Does he help firemen on Thursday?

5 Does he help animals on Friday?

6 Does he help children on Saturday?

2 Choose and write.

go   do   visit   ~~have~~   play   go

1

2

3

4

5

6

1 I ...... have ...... breakfast at ...... seven ...... o'clock.
2 I .... to school at .... o'clock.
3 I .... basketball at .... o'clock.
4 I .... my homework at .... o'clock.
5 I .... to the playground at .... o'clock.
6 I .... my grandma at .... o'clock.

What about you?

3 Draw and write about your day.

1 I get ....
at ....

2 I have ....
at ....

3 I go to ....
at ....

4 I do my ....
at ....

(1) Circle the food words.

(bread)   salad   cat   homework   pizza   snake   school

basketball   computer game   honey   chicken   eggs   dog   flower   milk   oranges

(2) Write.

I like ☺   I don't like ☹

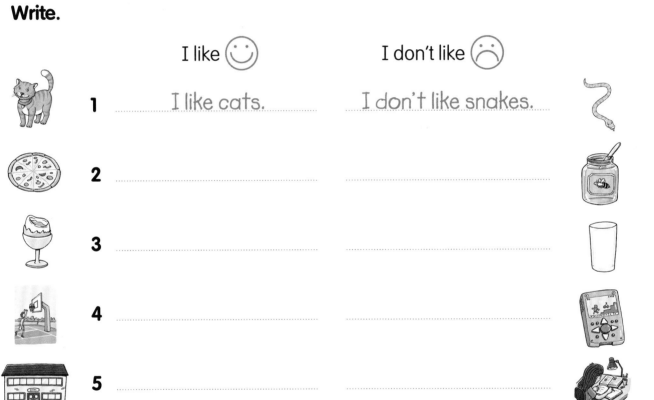

1   I like cats.   I don't like snakes.

2

3

4

5

(3) Match.

1 He cleans   a his breakfast.
2 She cleans   b up.
3 He gets   c to school.
4 He has   d her breakfast.
5 She has   e his teeth.
6 He goes   f her teeth.

3 **Choose and write the correct form.**

~~get up~~   have   go   like   play   go

Polly Pink is a dancer. She (**1**) gets up at nine o'clock every day. She (**2**) .... an apple and an orange for breakfast. She (**3**) .... apples. She doesn't like bread. She (**4**) .... to dancing school at eleven o'clock every day. After school, she (**5**) .... on her computer. She (**6**) .... to bed at ten o'clock.

4 **Look at Exercise 4. Write** Yes, she does **or** No, she doesn't.

1 Does Polly get up at nine o'clock every day?   Yes, she does.
2 Does she have eggs for breakfast?   ....
3 Does she like bread?   ....
4 Does she go to dancing school every day?   ....
5 Does she visit her grandma after school?   ....
6 Does she go to bed at ten o'clock?   ....

My English

Read and colour.

1 Do you like pizza?   ☺ ☺ ☺
   Yes, I do. / No, I don't.

2 Do you get up at seven o'clock?   ☺ ☺ ☺
   Yes, I do. / No, I don't.

3 Does your friend play basketball on Monday?   ☺ ☺ ☺
   Yes, he does. / No, he doesn't.

I'm playing a game!

1 Find, circle and match.

1

h	q	c	d	r	i	d	e
i	f	a	p	l	a	y	u
d	l	r	h	k	d	v	c
e	y	r	i	z	x	y	l
e	q	y	r	e	a	d	i
s	s	l	e	e	p	s	m
k	a	x	i	p	c	i	b
i	g	c	o	m	e	k	k
p	v	r	a	t	e	r	g

10

9

8

2

3  **4**  **5**  **6**  **7**

2 Choose and write.

reading   ~~writing~~   playing   hiding   sleeping

1 .... I'm writing. ....

2 ....

3 ....

4 ....

5 ....

3 **Look and write.**

~~reading~~ writing hiding playing sleeping doing

1 She's _reading_ a book.

2 He's _____ .

3 _____ a game.

4 _____ .

5 _____ .

6 _____ her homework.

4 **Match.**

1 I'm doing   **a** a big box.

2 He's playing   **b** a book.

3 She's riding   **c** my homework.

4 My dad is carrying   **d** my kite.

5 I'm flying   **e** her bike.

6 He's climbing   **f** her guitar.

7 My mum is reading   **g** a game.

8 Sally's playing   **h** a tree.

22 They're having a shower.

1 **Choose and write.**

~~dress~~   trousers   shoes   T-shirt   sweater

1 ....dress.......

2 ....

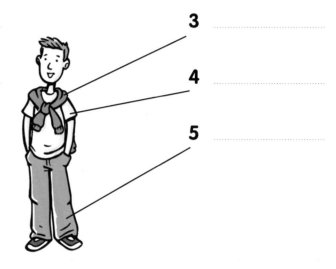

3 ....

4 ....

5 ....

2 **Look at Exercise 1 and write** yes **or** no.

1 She's wearing shoes. ......yes......
2 She's wearing a T-shirt. ....
3 She's wearing a sweater. ....
4 He's wearing a T-shirt. ....
5 He's wearing a dress. ....
6 He's wearing shoes. ....

3 **Read and colour.**

Sally is wearing a blue T-shirt and red trousers.
She's wearing yellow shoes.

4 **Circle, choose and write.**

hiding   ~~playing~~   sleeping   reading   doing their homework   having a shower

1 We're / (They're) .... playing ....

2 We're / They're ....

3 We're / They're ....

4 We're / They're ....

5 We're / They're ....

6 We're / They're ....

5 **Match.**

1	Chatter and Trumpet	**a**	We
2	Chatter and I	**b**	They
3	Sally and Patty	**c**	They
4	Tag and I	**d**	They
5	Karla and I	**e**	We
6	Tag and Karla	**f**	We

23 They aren't swimming!

1 Do the crossword.

volleyball   tennis   football   swimming   ~~basketball~~

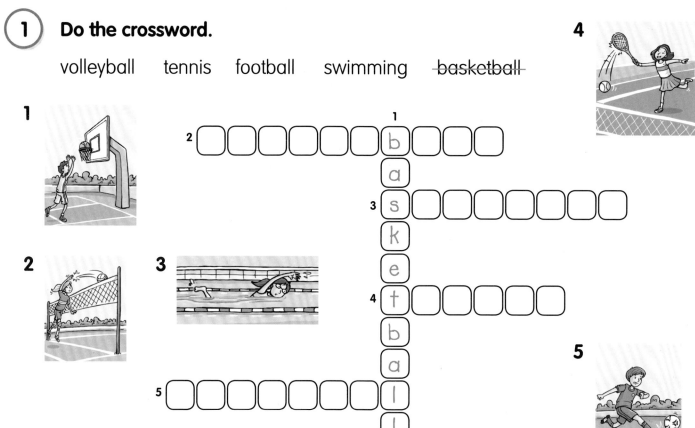

2 Circle.

1

She's reading. /
She isn't reading.

2

She's eating. /
She isn't eating.

3

She's playing
tennis. /
She isn't
playing tennis.

4

I'm swimming. /
I'm not swimming.

3 **Write. Use** He's, She's, He isn't **or** She isn't.

1

She's playing tennis.

2

.... playing football.

3

.... playing tennis.

4

.... playing football.

4 **Look and write.**

1 The rabbits ......_aren't playing_...... volleyball. They're ....
2 The ducks .... basketball. ....
3 The frogs .... football. ....

 **Are they sleeping?**

1 **Choose and write.**

~~roaring~~   snoring   drinking   dreaming

1

The lion ...is roaring.. .

2

The lion ....

3

The lion ....

4

The lion ....

2 **Circle.**

1

Are you swimming?
(Yes, we are.) /
No, we aren't.

2

Is she doing her
homework?
Yes, she is. /
No, she isn't.

3

Are you wearing
new shoes?
Yes, I am. /
No, I'm not.

4

Are they wearing
trousers?
Yes, they are. /
No, they aren't.

3 Write Is or Are.

1 __Is__ he reading his book?
2 _____ we doing our homework?
3 _____ she playing in the garden?
4 _____ they swimming?
5 _____ he dreaming?
6 _____ you writing?

4 Match.

1 Are you doing your homework?
2 Is he wearing a T-shirt?
3 Is she playing tennis?
4 Are we hiding?
5 Are they playing football?

a No, he isn't.
b No, you aren't.
c No, they aren't.
d No, I'm not.
e No, she isn't.

5 Write the questions in the correct order. Then answer.

1 the lion / sleeping? / Is

Is the lion sleeping?

No, it isn't. It's roaring.

2 she / Is / eating?

3 Are / playing / the boys / football?

4 doing / they / their homework? / Are

Jane and the giant

1 Read and answer.

1 Is Jane in the bedroom?
No, she isn't.

2 Is she hiding under the table?

3 Is Jane in the bathroom?

4 Is she hiding in a cupboard?

5 Is Jane in the kitchen?

6 Is she hiding in the shower?

7 Is Jane in the bathroom?

8 Is she hiding in the bed?

2 Find the odd one out. Write.

1 cupboard   table   bed   garden   garden

2 tennis   football   kitchen   volleyball

3 shoes   dress   T-shirt   bathroom

4 dream   giant   drink   eat

3 Complete.

1 I'm in the ba _____ room.

2 I'm in the k ____ t ____ en.

3 I'm in the l ____ v i ____ room.

4 I'm in the g _____ d ____ n.

What about you?

4 Look, write and colour. Then draw and write about you.

I'm not wearing _____ a skirt _____ .
I'm _____ a dress.
I'm wearing black trousers.
I'm _____ a T-shirt.
I'm _____ a red and blue sweater.

I'm not wearing _____ .
I'm wearing _____

_____ .
I'm not wearing _____ .
I'm wearing _____

_____ .

① **Write the words in the correct box.**

bathroom ~~basketball~~ trousers football kitchen shoes bedroom
volleyball living room dress skirt tennis

Sports	Rooms of the house	Clothes
basketball		

② **Write.**

1 My brother and I are . ...We're playing tennis.............

2 My friends are . ...

3 Sally is . ...

4 My dad is . ...

5 I am . ...

3 Match.

1 Is he dreaming?
2 Are you playing football?
3 Are they eating?
4 Is she sleeping?
5 Are we reading?
6 Is it drinking?

a No, she isn't.
b Yes, they are.
c Yes, he is.
d No, you aren't.
e No, it isn't.
f Yes, I am.

4 Write.

My mum is in the (**1**) ___kitchen___ . She's eating. My dad and my brother are in the garden. They're playing (**2**) _____ . I'm having a shower in the (**3**) _____ . My sister is in her (**4**) _____ . She's reading. My grandma is in the (**5**) _____ . She's writing. My grandpa is in his (**6**) _____ . He's sleeping.

My English

Read and colour.

1 Are you wearing a red sweater? Yes, I am. / No, I'm not.

2 Is your friend reading a book? Yes, he is. / No, he isn't.

3 In my home, there are three bedrooms.

25 These are crabs.

1 Circle.

1 This is a dolphin / turtle.　　**2** These are fish / crabs.　　**3** These are dolphins / rabbits.

4 These are fish / turtles.　　**5** This is a camera / photo.　　**6** This is a camera / photo.

2 Circle.

1 This is / These are her rabbits.　　　**2** This is / These are his dog.

3 This is / These are his turtles.　　　**4** This is / These are her fish.

3 **Write** This is **or** These are.

1   These are my rollerblades.

2   _____ my bike.

3   _____ my clothes.

4   _____ my watch.

5   _____ my presents.

4 **Write and answer. Use** Yes, it is, No, it isn't, Yes, they are **or** No, they aren't.

1   Are these your pencils?   Yes, they are .

2   Is this your _____?   No, _____ .

3   Are these your _____?   _____

4   Is this your _____?   _____

5   Are these your _____?   _____

6   Are these your _____?   _____

26 There are lots of people.

1 Find, circle and write.

p	e	o	p	l	e	q	w
r	g	c	i	t	a	e	o
o	i	l	a	q	h	p	m
t	r	m	a	n	g	z	a
y	l	n	u	b	o	y	n
e	q	w	i	x	f	r	p
c	h	i	l	d	r	e	n

1 people   **2** _____

3 _____   **4** _____   **5** _____   **6** _____

2 Choose and write.

old   tall   happy   slow   long   ~~short~~   fast   sad   new   short

1 He's   short   .
He's _____ .

2 It's _____ .
It's _____ .

3 It's _____ .
It's _____ .

4 It's _____ .
It's _____ .

5 He's _____ .
He's _____ .

3 Write the plurals.

box   ~~shark~~   dress   spy   crab   watch   baby   family   turtle

+ –s	+ –es	~~y~~ + –ies
sharks		

4 Look, count and write.

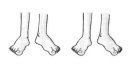

1 ...two... men   **2** .... women   **3** .... teeth   **4** .... feet

5 Write.

1 There are three ...babies... .

2 She's got white ....

3 He's got big ....

4 There are lots of .... at the zoo.

5 The .... are wearing pretty  ....

6 The .... are wearing ....

27 There are some apples.

1 Choose and write. Then colour.

~~bowl~~   sweet   carrot   chocolate   cherry

1 ......bowl......

2 ....

3 ....

4 ....

5 ....

2 Choose and write.

~~next to~~   in   on   under   on

1 I'm looking for my guitar.
It's ...next to... the cupboard.

2 I'm looking for my shoes.
They're .... the cupboard.

3 I'm looking for the sweets.
They're .... the drawer.

4 I'm looking for my camera.
It's .... the cupboard.

5 I'm looking for the cake.
It's .... the shelf.

3 **Look and write** are some **or** aren't any.

1 There _____are some_____ bananas in the bowl.

2 There _____ sweets in the bowl.

3 There _____ cherries in the bowl.

4 There _____ apples in the bowl.

5 There _____ eggs in the cupboard.

6 There _____ sweets in the cupboard.

7 There _____ cakes in the cupboard.

8 There _____ carrots in the cupboard.

4 **Answer about you. Write** Yes, there are **or** No, there aren't.

1 Are there any sweets in your bag? ....

2 Are there any pencils on your desk? ....

3 Are there any toys in your classroom? ....

4 Are there any books in your bedroom? ....

5 Are there any flowers in your garden? ....

6 Are there any swimming pools in your town? ....

1 **Circle.**

1 11 ⟨eleven⟩ seventeen eighteen
2 13 three thirteen eleven
3 14 twenty twelve fourteen
4 15 fourteen five fifteen
5 17 thirteen fifteen seventeen
6 19 nine nineteen ten
7 20 thirteen twenty sixteen

2 **Write and find the number.**

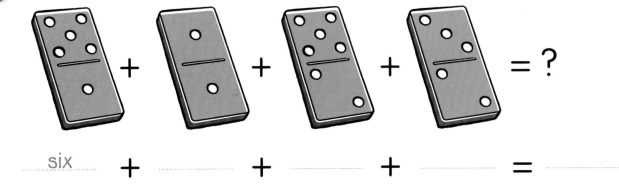

six + ... + ... + ... = ...

3 **Write the numbers.**

+	10	....	7
8	eighteen	twenty	fifteen
....	fifteen	seventeen	twelve
6	sixteen	eighteen	thirteen
....	thirteen	fifteen	ten

4 **Choose and write. Then answer.**

flowers   ~~ducks~~   frogs   insects   trees

1 How many .... ducks are there .... ? ....five....

2 How many .... ? ....

3 How many .... ? ....

4 How many .... ? ....

5 How many .... ? ....

5 **Match.**

1 How old are you?   **a** It's on the table.
2 What's your favourite food?   **b** I've got one.
3 Who's he?   **c** I'm eight.
4 How many brothers have you got?   **d** They're my books.
5 Where's your book?   **e** He's my dad.
6 What are these?   **f** Pizza.

Harry and Greta

1 Cross out the incorrect sentence.

1
a Harry and Greta see a beautiful house.
b There are sweets in the house.
c ~~Harry and Greta are sad.~~

2
a The old woman has got Harry.
b Harry has got a cake.
c Harry isn't happy.

3
a The squirrels eat the house.
b The old woman is angry.
c The squirrels eat the trees.

4
a Greta and Harry are happy.
b The old woman is in the town.
c The old woman is angry.

2 **Choose and write. Use** He's **or** She's**.**

hungry   tired   happy   funny   angry   ~~sad~~

1 ....He's sad........

2 ....

3 ....

4 ....

5 ....

6 ....

What about you?

3 **Look, read and write. Then draw and write about your home.**

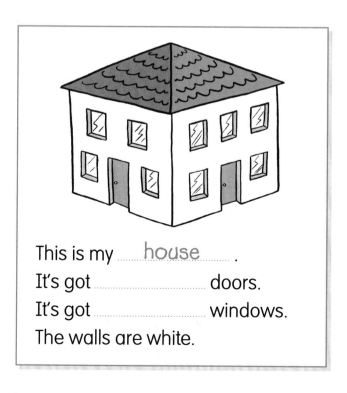

This is my ....house........ .
It's got .... doors.
It's got .... windows.
The walls are white.

This is *my* ....
It's got ....
....
....

1 **Read and colour.**

1 Number eleven has got black shoes.
2 Number nineteen has got a blue bag.

3 Number sixteen has got a red T-shirt.
4 Number twelve has got an orange ball.

2 **Write** What's this **or** What are these **and match.**

1

.... What's this? ....

a It's a camera.

2
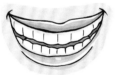
....

b They're cherries.

3

....

c It's a photo.

4

....

d It's a drawer.

5

....

e They're teeth.

3 **Write** There are some **or** There aren't any.

1 ___There aren't any___ crabs.
2 _____ turtles.
3 _____ families.

4 _____ sharks.
5 _____ fish.
6 _____ penguins.

4 **Circle and answer about you.**

1 Who / (What) is your favourite colour?

_____

2 How old / How many are you?

_____

3 Who / What is your teacher?

_____

4 What / Where is your school bag?

_____

5 How many / Where people are there in your family?

_____

My English

Read and colour.

1 What's this? It's a dolphin. What are these? They're crabs. 😐 🙂 😀

2 There are some books in my bag. There aren't any sweets. 😐 🙂 😀

3 How many pencils are there? There are twelve. 😐 🙂 😀

Pearson Education Limited
Edinburgh Gate
Harlow
Essex CM20 2JE
England
and Associated Companies throughout the world.

www.pearsonelt.com

First published 2010
Twenty-first impression 2023

ISBN: 9781408248218

Printed in Slovakia by Neografia

Set in VagRounded

Ilustrated by: GS Animation/Grupa Smacznego
Christos Skaltsas/eyescream, Zaharias Papadopoulos/
eyescream, Katerina Chrysohoou, Victor Moschopoulos/
chickenworks
Digital illustrations by: HL Studios, Long Hanborough, Oxford

Acknowledgements
The publishers and authors would like to thank all the
consultants, schools and teachers who helped to develop this
course for their valuable feedback and comments.